PAPER PERFECT

PAPER PERFECT

25 BRIGHT IDEAS FOR PAPER

LABEENA ISHAQUE

LARK BOOKS

DEDICATION

For my sister, Sameena Ishaque

ACKNOWLEDGEMENTS

Thank you to Lesley Tomlin and Penny Duke at Paperchase for their time, generosity and assistance; Venetia Penfold and Janine Hosegood, my editor and the photographer, both of whom I loved working with, and to my friends Azi, Martin, Libby and Jane who all helped in various ways.

PUBLISHERS' ACKNOWLEDGEMENTS

The publishers would like to thank Labeena Ishaque for her creative contribution to the styled photography and to the following for generously lending props for photography: Paperchase, 213 Tottenham Court Road, London W1P 9AF; Nice Irma's, 46 Goodge Street, London W1P 1FJ; Muji, 187 Oxford Street, London W1R 1AJ; Miss Selfridge, Ten Hill Place, London W1R 1AF.

Library of Congress Cataloging-in-Publication Data Available

10 9 8 7 6 5 4 3 2 1

Published by Lark Books
50 College St.
Asheville, NC 28801, USA

Distributed by Random House, Inc., in the United States and Canada
First published in 1998 by B T Batsford Ltd., London

Text and designs © 1998 Labeena Ishaque
The moral right of the author has been asserted.
Photographs and illustrations © B T Batsford

Every effort has been made to ensure that all the information in this book is accurate. However, due to differing conditions, tools, and individual skills, the publisher cannot be responsible for any injuries, losses, or other damages that may result from the use of the information in this book.

Printed in China

Photography by Janine Hosegood
Color illustrations by Robert Highton
Designed by DWN Ltd., London

ISBN 1–57990–076–3

Contents

introduction

While paper is still the most popular medium for communication, it has so much more potential than as just a material for writing and drawing on. It may seem a very humble material to many people, but its rich and varied qualities and its long history give it a functional, as well as a cultural significance.

The process of making paper is so simple, consisting of pulping fibres in water, pouring the pulp into a frame and allowing it to dry. It requires very little specialist equipment, and time and patience are more important than any creative talent. Quite simply, the more paper you make, the more proficient you will become, but at the same time your very first attempt should give you surprising and pleasing results.

This book gives a brief introduction to making paper, and then concentrates on what wonders can be made with both handmade and shop-bought papers! Paper as a decorative and structural material has immense possibilities and these are explored by the projects throughout this book. Just by flicking through the following pages you will discover just how creative and versatile working with paper can be.

Labeena Ishaque

A Brief History of Paper

Since the beginning of time, mankind has looked for a way to record events. Early records, using natural materials such as chalk and ochre, have been found on cave walls and clay and stone tablets, providing us with invaluable evidence about mankind's history. As time passed, a more practical and portable form of recording events and written communication was required. Animal skin, as an easily portable flat surface, was the earliest form of 'paper' to be used and parchment (sheepskin treated with lime), and vellum (calf or goat skin), were developed from this method of communication.

Papyrus, the closest ancestor to the paper of today, was linked with the Ancient Egyptians, who used a grass-like plant to make sheets for writing.

The papyrus stalk was split into layers which were then flattened out, using water to act as glue and hold the strips at right angles to each other to form a sheet. These sheets were then pressed, beaten flat and dried in the sun.

As early as the second century AD, the process of making paper was being refined in parts of Central America and the Pacific Islands. The inner fibers from tree barks and cloth were beaten until thin and these were sewn together and decorated with pigments.

Up until this time, the Chinese had been using either fine cloth or rice paper, an ancient form of paper in China which is made from tree pith. This is peeled from the tree in one long, continuous thin length, which is dampened and dried flat. The Chinese then invented a technique for producing a material, similar to what we now recognize as paper and this was applied widely to everyday life in China.

The discovery of paper spread through Nepal, Japan, India, Arabia, North Africa and Spain. The technique had reached Europe by the twelfth century, arriving eventually in England in the late fifteenth century. The East and West developed different techniques for paper-making. The 'laid' mold technique of India and China used a frame made with fine grasses, so that semi-translucent lines would appear on the finished sheet, and the 'woven' mold technique of the West, used a woven, mesh-like frame, giving close, even textures on the papers.

The invention of the paper-making machine in the late eighteenth century hailed the production of paper as a huge industry. This resulted in its increased availability, resulting in its use for diverse purposes from newspapers, to books and packaging. Mass production has accentuated differences in quality between handmade and machine-made papers. Machine-made papers are much weaker, because the fibers of the paper lie in one direction only, whereas a good handmade sheet of paper can last hundreds of years.

The paper industry needs trees for its raw materials and the sheer volume of our consumption is destroying the world's forests – this in turn destroys the natural food chains of the animal kingdom, as well as the atmosphere surrounding the earth which protects us. Sustainable forests are now being grown specifically for paper and it is important for each of us to make our own contribution towards the recycling of paper waste.

With the widespread use of electronic media, such as telephones, the Internet and E-mail, paper will not be so crucial in the future. Once eliminated as a mass-produced and throwaway item, then it can gain its rightful place as a beautiful, tactile, creative material which should be enjoyed and treasured.

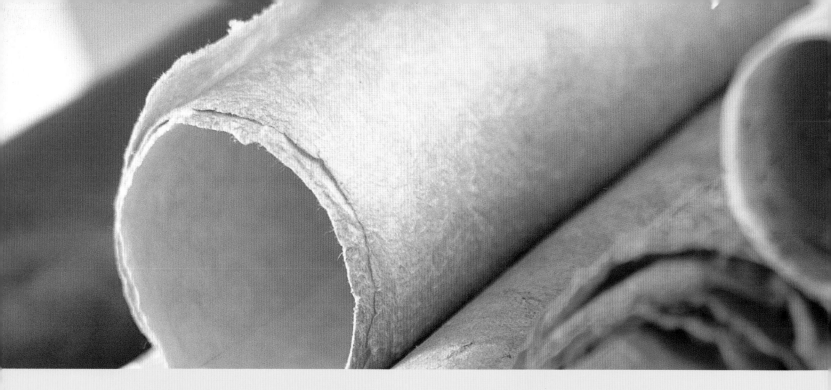

CHAPTER 1

Materials and

Basic Techniques

Papermaking Materials

Before you can begin making paper, you will need to check if you have the right equipment to use in your experiments. The great thing about making paper and the equipment needed is that they are so accessible – most of the materials can be found around your home, allowing you to try it out without investing in a vast range of equipment.

Apart from the mold and deckle, which are the frame and base tools used to form sheets of paper out of the pulp, all the other equipment, such as basins, buckets, saucepans and sieves, can be found in your kitchen or laundry room. In fact even the mold and deckle can be made relatively simply and at a fraction of the retail cost using old picture frames or thin lengths of wood.

Papermaking is quite a messy business, so it does pay to be organised and get all the materials that you might need prepared before you start work. It is also a very spontaneous craft, allowing you to work intuitively with different materials (the Techniques section discusses how to create different sorts of papers with various materials, such as plant fibers or unusual textures). If you are interested in experimenting in this way, it is certainly a good idea to keep an eye out for any interesting materials to incorporate in your homemade paper, or tools and textures with which to manipulate the paper while it is being made (see page 20) and once it is dry (see page 22).

PLASTIC TUB OR WASHING-UP BOWL

It is important to have a couple of bowls. They can be used as containers for soaking scrap paper to make the pulp, to pour the pulp into once it has been made, to use as a vat when dipping the mold and deckle into the pulp or as drip trays to catch any excess water.

PLASTIC SHEETS AND BUCKET

Making paper is a very wet business, so these are useful for protecting surfaces and for carrying water to and from the work surface.

FOOD LIQUIDIZER

This is used to pound the soaked papers and fibers into a mashed pulp. Before being liquidized, the scrap papers or fibers are cut or torn into small pieces and are soaked in water overnight.

MOLD AND DECKLE

These are two equal size frames (Fig. 1) – a letter size is the ideal size for a beginner as it fits comfortably in a washing-up bowl. Smaller sheets of paper are also much easier to handle at the beginning. The mold is a frame with mesh stretched over it and the deckle is a frame which lies on top of the mold. The sheet of paper is formed on the mold and the deckle shapes the sheet.

Fig. 1

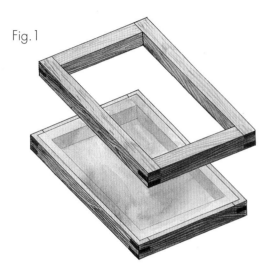

If you decide to make your own mold and deckle, old picture frames can be easily adapted for this purpose. Otherwise simply make two frames from 1 x 1 cm (⅜ x ⅜ in) sections of wood and then pin or staple the corners and strengthen them with L-shaped metal plates. Cover the frame which you have chosen for the mold with mesh, staple the mesh to one of the shorter sides first, then stretch it across to the opposite side and staple the two longer sides last of all. The kind of mesh you use is not crucial – aluminium and brass mesh are long-lasting, but curtain or nylon netting can be just as effective. If you are going to use fabric, ensure that you dampen it before stretching it across the frame, so that it does not distort when the pulp lies on it.

SIEVE, COLANDER AND NETTING

These can be used for straining excess water out of the pulp before pouring it onto the mold.

LARGE STAINLESS STEEL SAUCEPAN

This is only needed if you want to make pulp from tougher plant materials, in which case they need to be boiled for a while to soften them.

MALLET

This is used to pound the plant fibers into a more manageable consistency when making pure plant papers.

LAUNDRY STARCH

This can be added to the plant or paper pulp mixture to stop it from being too absorbent. Gelatin can also be used for this purpose.

PVA OR WHITE GLUE

A teaspoon of PVA added to the pulp mixture with the starch or gelatin will also prevent the finished paper from being too absorbent.

OLD BLANKETS AND ALL-PURPOSE CLOTHS

These are used to dry the paper on – old blankets are ideal for soaking out excess water and they can be used with newspaper as a blotting device.

TWO LARGE BOARDS

When the paper is almost dry, boards can be used to press and flatten off the sheets.

Basic Techniques

TRADITIONAL METHODS

The main processes for making paper are mixing the pulp, making the sheets and then couching, which is removing the sheets and allowing them to dry.

MAKING THE PULP

This is the first stage in paper-making and it is a really simple process. The beauty of making paper at home is that you can recycle your old scrap paper to create new and exciting papers in varying thicknesses, sizes, textures and colors. Most papers to be found lying around the home and office can be used to make the pulp.

Newspaper is ideal for use as the bulk of your paper pulp, but note that white newspapers tend to go grey, whereas pink newspapers become beige or brown. Avoid fax paper and glossy magazines, as these are very shiny and have a high acid content which means that finished paper sheets will become yellow and brittle and may not last very long. Do not use paper with too much black print, or alternatively remove the print by simply putting a few drops of detergent, such as dishwashing liquid, into the water while pulping. When you add detergent to this mixture a scum will form at the top of the pulp, but this can be scraped off the top and washed out with water.

The best papers to use are photocopying and typing papers which are much stronger than newspapers and are generally white, resulting in a soft, creamy white color pulp. If you visit local offices, colleges or schools and ask for their scrap paper, most will surely be happy to see it going to good use.

Brown packaging paper, carrier bags, old envelopes and notebooks also provide good material. This may sound obvious, but the higher the quality of paper used in the pulp, the better the finished handmade papers will be, so it is a good idea to add some good-quality cotton linter paper to your pulp mixture which will toughen it up. Cotton linter paper is a paper with very long fibers, much longer than the fibers in recycled papers, so it adds strength to a pulp mixture. Experiment with these papers before pulping them, to find out what colors will result once they have been pounded. Do this by tearing off a little section and soaking it in water, then squeezing it up in your hands and allowing it to dry. Experimenting in this way is bound to result in some unexpected and unusual effects.

MATERIALS
Scrap paper
Water
Washing-up bowls
Blender
Airtight containers
A spoonful of PVA or white glue
A tablespoon of laundry starch

METHOD

1 Tear the papers up into small squares no larger than 5 cm (2 in) and soak them in water overnight in a large bowl. For a quicker result, boil them in a large saucepan for about half an hour.

2 Once the paper is soggy and is retaining water, then proceed to liquify the pulp in a blender. Do this for about ten seconds on a high setting, just adding a small amount of pulp at a time.

3 Blend the pulp until it is quite smooth and creamy with the consistency of thick soup and mix in the PVA and the starch. Do not blend the pulp for too long at this stage as the more it is broken up, the shorter the paper fibers will be and this will result in a weaker finished sheet of paper.

Note: A thick consistency pulp is easier to start off with as a beginner. However the fact of the matter is that the thinner the pulp, the finer and more delicate the finished sheet of paper will be, so as you gain confidence start to thin the pulp mixture.

4 The pulp can be stored in an airtight container, but when left for too long it will start to smell unpleasant, so aim to make only as much as you need each time. Pulp can also be squeezed out and stored dry, however it will need liquidizing with water before it is used.

USING PLANT FIBERS

Many different kinds of plant materials can be used to mix into a pulp of scrap paper – onion skins, leeks, reeds, celery, any kind of leaves and flowers, flax, cotton or soft plant stalks. A wander around your garden will give you untold possibilities for paper-making experiments.

Smaller plants and flowers can be thrown into the blender and simply added to the pulp. The softer stalks, too, can be added straight to the pulp, but these are best when they have just been picked so that they are at their most malleable. Tiny flowers and leaves can be added straight to the pulp and mixed in without liquidizing to make decorative papers, but it is important to then make sure that these papers are pressed and dried flat with weights and boards, as the finished paper can be very delicate and brittle.

Thai purple petal paper (adding plant fibers)

MAKING PULP FROM PLANTS

This is a little more time consuming, especially when they are tougher and consist of many strands and twisted fibers, such as celery, leeks, pampas grass, nettles, rush and straw.

MATERIALS
Plant fibers
Water
Large, stainless steel saucepan
Large colander
Blender
Airtight container
Netting
Scissors
Mallet

METHOD
1 Cut the plant fibers into 4–5 cm (1⅝–2 in) strips and boil these in the large saucepan until the fibers begin to break up into strands. Boil on a high heat for approximately two hours and keep adding water if necessary to ensure that the fibers become quite soft.

2 When the fibers are soft and quite slimy to the touch, they are ready to be rinsed out. Wash the non-fibrous materials away with cool water.

3 Place a large colander in the sink and line it with the netting, then proceed to pour the plant fibers into it. Rinse it out further, squeezing the matter as you do so. Pull up the edges of the netting, gather them together to form a bag and squeeze out the excess water.

Note: If the plant materials are very tough, a little caustic soda could be added to the pan when boiling. This can damage the fibers, so try and avoid using this if possible. Always use rubber gloves when using chemicals like this and make sure the fibers are rinsed thoroughly to wash away the residue.

4 At this stage the plant material can either be added to the paper pulp or made into a pure plant pulp. If you want to add it to the paper pulp, simply introduce some of the fibers into the paper pulp, mixing the two together until they are thoroughly combined. Add a little of the plant fiber at a time, until you are satisfied with the proportions of the combination.

5 Alternatively a sheet of paper can be made from the pure plant pulp. The plant pulp needs to be laid on a flat surface with a little water and beaten with a mallet to soften and separate the fibers. This can be added to the blender, but I suggest that you beat them thoroughly with the mallet to feather and disintegrate the fibers, as the blender will break them into very short pieces, resulting in a weaker paper. Keep the mixture quite wet and add a touch of fabric conditioner to the pulp at this stage. The conditioner will assist couching and drying when the time comes, as longer fibers can be difficult to work with at later stages.

6 If the fibrous pulp is too dark, this can be lightened by adding a little bleach while pounding the mixture, but be sure to wear gloves to protect your hands if you do this. Place the pulp into an airtight container and, again, only make as much as you need.

MAKING SHEETS OF PAPER

Once the pulp has been made, the next stage is to form the sheets of paper. The procedure is the same for both paper and plant pulps.

MATERIALS
Pulp mixture
Plastic dishpan
Mold and deckle
Spare plastic bowls
Plastic sheets to cover work surfaces

METHOD

1 First of all place the pulp into a dishpan, filling it at least three-quarters full. Ensure that you agitate the pulp mixtures, as the bulk tends to settle at the bottom of the containers and the mixture does need to be even at this stage.

2 Place the deckle on top of the mold and hold them together firmly, at each short side. Immerse the mold and deckle vertically, with the deckle facing you, into the far end of the pan. Swing them horizontally, scooping up pulp as you do so, pulling them towards yourself slowly and smoothly (see Fig. 2).

Fig. 2

15

3 Keeping the mold and deckle flat, lift it out of the pulp. The pulp will be suctioned onto the mold and held in place. Give it a quick shake from side to side and forwards and backwards, until all the water has drained through the mold. This will disperse the fibers and even out the pulp (see Fig. 3)

Fig. 3

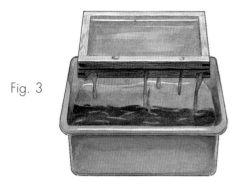

4 You will notice that the pulp will immediately begin to stiffen. Hold the mold and deckle over the bowl at a very slight angle and allow any excess water to drip out from one corner.

5 Place the mold and deckle on a flat surface, protected by a plastic sheet. Carefully lift the deckle away, trying not to let it drip onto the pulp sheet, as drips at this stage can spoil the paper.

6 If the sheet is badly formed – either lumpy or uneven – you can simply turn it upside down into the bowl, remix the pulp and try again.

7 Before you make the next sheet, remember to wash the mold and deckle, as pulp residue can cause unsightly lumps and bumps to appear on your paper.

The process of making paper is just as simple as that!

COUCHING

Once the pulp has been laid on the deckle and mould and the deckle removed, it is time to remove the pulp from the mold to dry and form your sheets of paper. This technique is traditionally called 'couching'.

MATERIALS
Large flat board
Jug of water
All-purpose cloths or interfacing
Old blankets cut to the same size as the
    board
Newspaper

METHOD

1 Lay the board down onto your work surface, lay the blanket on top of that and then the all-purpose cloth or interfacing on top of the pile, making sure that they are all lying smoothly with no creases. Pour water onto the cloth and blanket to make them quite wet – this is done so that they will not shrink or stretch when the wet pulp is placed on top of them. It will also aid the couching process by reducing the risk of the fibers in the pulp tearing when the dry paper is taken off the cloth.

2 Take away the deckle frame and stand the mold on one long side. Quickly, but carefully, invert the mold, holding the pulp onto the cloth while still wet. Tap the back of the mold without moving it and lift it off (see Fig. 4).

Fig. 4

3 If the pulp will not come off, leave the mold face down on the cloth, get a dry sponge and press it down over the exposed mesh. As the pulp absorbs the water a vacuum will be created, allowing you to pull the mold away slightly. The pulp should then pop off the mold and stick to the cloth.

From this point you can choose either to make multiple sheets at one size or one large sheet.

METHOD
(for multiple sheets)

1 Once you have made your first sheet, cover it with another piece of interfacing or cloth, scoop up more pulp in the freshly washed mold and deckle and place that on top of the second piece of interfacing.

2 Proceed to sandwich sheets of pulp and interfacing in a pile. This can be done half a dozen times, then finished off with another piece of old blanket at the top of the pile and a board on top of that, which can be weighed down to squeeze out any excess water and flatten the sheets.

METHOD
(for one large sheet)

1 Ensure that the board, blanket and cloth are large enough to hold the size of paper that you want to make. Place the first sheet of pulp on one side of the cloth, quickly fill the mold and deckle again, then place this next to the first sheet, allowing the edges to overlap.

2 Repeat this process until you have the size you require. Press these sheet together before drying, as it will strengthen the joins.

Once the sheets of pulp are ready, there are two ways to dry them:

- The sheets can be hung up on a clothesline, while still adhering to the cloth. Hang in a warm dry place and then simply peel away the cloth when the paper is dry.

- The second way is to board dry the pulp into paper. After pressing the pulp, lift up the pulp on the cloth, put the cloth pulp side down onto a large board and then brush the back of the cloth with a large dry brush or sponge. This will disturb the suction and allow the cloth to be peeled away easily.

PAPER CARE
There are a few 'common-sense' rules when you work with paper. When you are carrying paper, hold the corners at opposite sides and when transporting it, roll the paper loosely along the grain and into a tube. Never apply undue pressure when working with it, as the paper can bruise and buckle very quickly, as well as become shiny.

Right: Papers from top of pile
– Thai mixed petal paper;
Richard de Bas paper; Natural
papyrus; Handmade bleached
diamond paper; Handmade
cotton paper with marigold
and bouganvillea; Rain paper;
Handmade walnut; Japanese
asacukusui (pink); Mexican
bark (violet); Japanese ichima-
tusu (black); Banana paper;
Nautilus/ammonite Spanish
shell paper; Toscana embossed
paper; Rainbow paper;
Coconut paper (red);
Handmade crushed paper
(green); Nepalese tissue lokta
(blue).

18

CONTEMPORARY METHODS

CREATING TEXTURE WHEN PAPERMAKING

Texture can be added to the paper while it is being made, giving extra definition and interest to the surface. For the methods which follow, the texture is added while the pulp is still quite wet, before it dries into paper. The pulp is made in the same way as described on page 13, but the damp sheets are treated differently. Rather than allowing them to dry flat, texture is added while the pulp is malleable and easy to work into. This is where you can really let go and become tactile and intimate with the paper – remember that paper is not just for writing and drawing on, it does not have to be flat and regimented, but can be as swirly, patchy or contoured as you want it to be. There follow a variety of relatively simple ways to achieve unusual effects on paper.

DECKLESS

Removing the deckle from the paper-making process gives much greater scope for developing the shape and edge texture of paper. Do not restrict your work by always working within the traditional rectangular-shaped paper – the pulp can be moved around the mold by hand and rearranged to your own specifications. The edges of the paper can be finished off in a number of ways – pinched and raised to create tiny little scallops around the sheet, patterns sectioned off while the pulp is still damp with a spoon or a blunt knife or the pulp can be tapered to give the paper very fine edges.

WATERMARKS

Watermarks are slightly raised designs or motifs on paper. These motifs are actually attached to the mesh of the mold onto which the wet pulp is scooped. Attach a motif to your mold by incorporating wire into the mesh, using fine piano, fishing or florists' wire. These wires are looped onto the mesh by threading them through or by sewing them into place.

PATCHWORK PAPERS

This is another method without using the deckle. If you want to make a paper with very small patches then make small sheets, but only use one quarter or one eighth of the mold and leave the edges uneven and ragged, as this adds to the effect. Tip the first small patch onto the blanket and cloth, then proceed to make many more small patches, laying them all side by side and overlapping the edges to build up a patchwork. Pastry cutters could be used to make unusual shaped patches which can be worked together like a quilt. Using with two or three different colored or textured pulps will highlight the patching. When the patchwork has been built up, lay a board over the top and press to aid the strengthening of the joins.

COLLAGES

Collages can be made on newly formed sheets while they are still wet. Prepare the pulp in the deckle and mold and lay the sheet out on the cloth and blanket. Using the damp pulp as an adhesive, add other materials to give texture. Tiny strips or scraps of paper or pressed flower heads and leaves are examples of materials which can be laid onto the pulp. Also experiment with twine, strings, feathers and even tissue paper and stamps. The only restriction is needing to stick to very light and small objects, otherwise they will not adhere to the pulp.

EMBOSSING

Embossing can be done once the paper is actually dry (see page 28), but the results are so much better if done while the pulp is still damp, as a newly formed sheet of paper. The pulp is at its most malleable and easy to work with when it is still wet, so it picks up textures very quickly when pressed.

Fabrics like lace and netting give a really good result – lay them on a freshly made sheet, cover them with interfacing and an old blanket and then press beneath a board. Leave the fabric in place until the paper has dried and then peel it away.

ADDING COLOR

When most people begin making paper, the pulp is generally made from recycled paper, the bulk of which will probably be newspaper. There are two main types of newspaper: those printed on white paper and those printed on pink. White newspaper becomes a soft grey, whereas the pink becomes a creamy brown color.

If you have a range of colored papers to recycle as pulp, keep them together in groups, so that you can achieve some colors without adding it afterwards.

In order to vary the color shades of the natural state of the pulp, it can quite easily be colored further to make it more distinctive. A general rule to note when adding color to pulp is that the color should be added gradually. You can always add more color, but it is much more difficult to remove it. The pulp will also be darker in tone when it is wet and the true color will not become evident until it has dried, so make allowances for this when you are adding the color.

Make samples of the colored pulp before you proceed, by taking a pinch of dyed pulp, squeezing out the excess water and drying it quickly with a hairdryer or on a radiator to see the color result. Add more pulp if its too dark and more color if its too light.

FOOD COLORING

Add a few drops of food coloring to the pulp before or while it is being liquidized – this is so that the color is distributed through the mixture evenly. Food coloring is very strong, so only add one drop at first, blend and then gradually add more if you need to.

Oyster shell Spanish fossil paper (embossing pulp)

Rainbow paper (adding color)

FABRIC AND COLD-WATER DYES

These can also be added while liquidizing the pulp. However, these dyes do tend to stain, so you may prefer to mix the dyes with the pulp in a plastic bowl. If you do mix them in a bowl, the dyes need time to dissolve and disperse throughout the mixture. Again, only add a little at a time, as these dyes are very strong and you can often achieve the color that you want with a minimum amount of dye.

POWDER PAINTS AND INKS

Again, simply add pigments to the pulp, either in the blender or in a bowl. Allow them time to dissolve and disperse into the mixture. Agitate the mixture with a rod or stick before you scoop the pulp into the mold and deckle. An alternative way to use powder colors is to create a deliberate color pattern on the pulp – make a sheet of paper out of uncolored pulp, remove the sheet from the deckle and mold, then sprinkle the powder paints across the wet pulp. The paint will disperse a little, but not so much that it is not possible to control it. Try working it into patterns, lines, squares, borders and even monograms.

SPICES

Powdered spices like turmeric and paprika have the most wonderful, vibrant colours which can be used to dye paper. Stir a few spoonfuls of the spice into a little boiling water to help it dissolve and then add it to the pulp in the blender.

BLEACH

Once the paper has been made and dried, the paper can be bleached. This works well with natural-colored papers. For instance, a paper made from newspaper pulp will look grey, but this is easy to transform by painting undiluted bleach onto the surface, either blocking out sections or painting lines or waves to form a background patterned surface. Fabric dyes can also be worked into paper like this, or even wiped across the paper with a sponge.

STAMPING AND PRINTING

The surface of your handmade sheets of paper can be decorated in numerous ways, from painting and drawing to other decorating techniques. There are many ways of introducing a pattern or motif on the paper and stamping and printing are good techniques for creating a repeating pattern.

ADDING TEXTURE TO PAPER

Texture can be added to both handmade and shop-bought papers. Once you have the papers that you want to work with, there are a number of ways that they can be treated to give them further textures. Before beginning to work with your papers, there are a number of points to note regarding the paper's fiber and grain.

FIBER AND GRAIN

All manufactured papers and cards have a grain. The grain is formed by the way the fibers in the pulp lie in the sheet; when papers are made in a machine, the belt pulls the pulp from the wet end to the dry end, making the fibers lie in one particular direction. Handmade papers tend not to have a grain, as they are made in a mold and this allows the fibers to lie quite randomly.

Before embarking on any of the following paper techniques – especially folding, tearing and creasing – find out in which direction the grain is lying so that you can work with it. If this is not done, the folds and tears will be uneven and rough.

Test the direction of the grain, simply by bending the sheet of paper in half (without folding or creasing it). Do this several times to test how it springs. Then turn the paper around by 90 degrees and repeat the process. You will notice a difference in the tension – the sheet bends more easily along the grain, and it will be harder to work with the paper against the grain as it just does not have the same flexibility.

The grain direction can also be established by creasing a piece of paper sharply, both along the grain and against it. The fold along the grain will be smooth and sharp and the fold against it will be broken and jagged. If you tear paper along the grain, it will tear in a smooth strip, if you tear it against the grain, it is difficult to tear in one piece and will look rather messy.

FOLDING AND CREASING

Although a very simple and accessible technique, folding paper can give very different and exciting results. The technique can be used both as a decorative feature, or to create a paper structure.

MATERIALS
A smooth, round-ended implement to use as a folding utensil (such as a bone folder, letter opener or a narrow handle of a knife)
Metal ruler
Soft pencil and eraser

METHOD
1 Work out the direction of the grain and then measure and mark the top, middle and bottom of the required folds with a pencil, so that the ruler lies at a right angle to the edge of the paper.

2 Using the ruler and the folding utensil, fold the paper up and score the paper, sandwiching it between the ruler and the utensil (see Fig. 5).

3 Take the ruler out and fold again to strengthen the fold. Proceed to make creases in this manner, by flipping the paper to make a crease on the other side. The possibilities of folds and creases are endless by alternating the sizes and patterns.

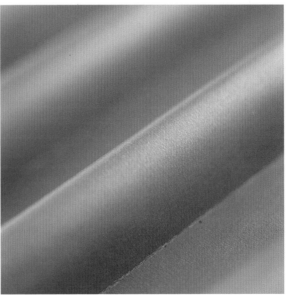

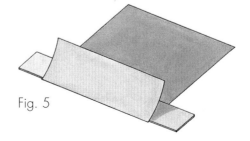

Fig. 5

CURLING, ROLLING AND FLUTING

When fluting and rolling paper, you need to work with the grain of the paper, otherwise the paper will buckle and mark. If the paper is rolled with the grain, it can be made into tight, even cylinders, which will have significantly more strength in them.

Rolling needs no instruction, as it is simply a case of holding the paper and rolling from one side to the opposite end and then securing it. Fluting is carried out with two pieces of paper, one to make the flutes and another to support them.

MATERIALS
Sheet of paper
Stiff paper or card as the support
Folding utensil
Paper glue
Paperclips
Ruler
Pencil

METHOD

1 Measure and mark the paper where you would like the fluting to be, remembering that once the flutes stand up, they will be narrower than the marks. Keep this in mind when measuring the folds, by creasing it again backwards and forwards.

2 Clip the parts that you intend to keep flat onto the backing paper at the top and bottom edges. Then ease the flutes into place, as high or as low as you wish. Once this is done, then go ahead and glue the flat strips onto the backing paper (see Fig. 6).

Fig. 6

CUTTING AND TEARING

Cutting and tearing paper gives a number of textural possibilities, depending on how it is done. Methods of cutting not only include cutting from the edges of the paper, but also ways in which pieces, such as small holes, flaps or windows, can be cut out.

MATERIALS
Metal ruler
Cutting mat
Sharp craft knife

METHOD
(for cutting paper)

1 Hold the ruler down on the paper, slightly at an angle to yourself, so that you are not cutting towards yourself. Push the blade deep into the paper and cut in one long stroke, so as to avoid jagged edges.

2 Small cuts and cutouts can be very effective on large sheets of paper. Slits and windows that allow light to pass through them are ideal for making lampshades and shades for night lights (see Golden Lanterns on page 38).

METHOD
(for tearing paper)

1 It is advisable to tear along the grain to give a cleaner break and even strips. Place a ruler down on the paper along the grain and simply tear the paper off to create regular edges or strips. If you would like more irregular pieces, then go ahead and tear across the paper.

2 Practice on scrap pieces of paper first and you will soon see that papers will react differently. Thicker papers have many layers, so you need to adjust the way you are tearing to accommodate this.

WEAVING

By cutting slits or narrow rectangular shapes out of a sheet of paper, in rows and at intervals, passages are made that allow strips of paper to be passed through, creating a woven effect. Simply mark off equal-sized slits along the length of a piece of paper, then using a metal ruler and a sharp craft knife, cut slits through the paper. Cut a strip of paper slightly narrower than the slits and thread it in and out of them to make a weave. This can be done in single rows to give small details, or an entire sheet of paper could be threaded.

Another way to create a woven effect is to actually weave strips of paper together to form a sheet, rather than threading strips through a sheet. Once the basics of this have been picked up, you can experiment with different sized strips and different colors and patterns to make checks, plaids and tartans. This kind of textured paper can be used to make decorative features on greetings cards and stationery, as well as more practical objects, such as the lampshade on page 46, which is made from woven tissue paper. Tissue papers also add depth to the weave because the transparent qualities allow a second color to show through the first. The method for weaving a sheet of paper is shown here.

MATERIALS
Craft knife
Metal ruler
Cutting mat
Masking tape
Pencil

METHOD

1   Select the paper you wish to use for the warp section of the weave (the upright part of the weave). Mark the paper to the width that you would like the strips to be and then cut them using a craft knife. Start the cuts about 2 cm (¾ in) from the top, to look like a long fringe which will keep the strips together and parallel. If you cut across the grain the woven structure will be kept as rigid as possible.

2   Cut the strips that will be woven across the weft section (the horizontal part of the weave) and simply proceed to weave these through the warp, pushing them up so that they lie side by side. Once they have been woven to the end of the warp, secure the ends with tape (see Fig. 7).

27

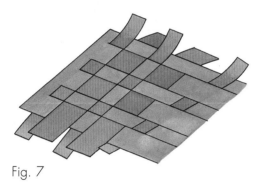

Fig. 7

PIERCING

Piercing paper with any number of implements will give unusual and varied textures to any kind of paper. Large holes can be made using hole punches, whereas tiny individual dots can be made with sewing, darning and knitting needles. A dressmaker's wheel can also be used to create rows of closely joined holes.

The only materials needed for this technique are the paper, the right needle or wheel and a yielding surface to lay the paper on, so that it can be perforated easily (an old piece of blanket is ideal for this). There is an immense variety of pattern possibilities for this technique, from rows and criss-cross checks to motifs. Create motifs by drawing on the paper lightly with a pencil and then tracing around the line with the needle, leaving small spaces in between each perforation.

EMBOSSING AND IMPRESSING

Although this is best done while making the paper (see page 20), it can be done with any paper, providing it is not too thick. Embossing is an easy process, involving making a deep impression on the paper with a shape or motif.

MATERIALS
Water spray
Waterproof board
Weights or paper press
Objects to use for impressing

METHOD
1 Dampen the paper by spraying it evenly with water until it is soft (try not to make it too wet as this can distort it).

2 Select the motif or shape you want to impress, draw it on very thick card and cut it out. Alternatively you can use objects with shapes built into them, such as netting, string, beans, rice or even wire shaped into a motif or pattern.

3 Lay the item onto a hard, waterproof surface and then lay the damp paper on top of that. Cover this with a double thickness of old blanket, as the thicker the fabric layer, the more easily and quickly the impression can be made. Once the blanket has been laid down, cover this with a flat board and proceed to weigh it down with heavy weights or a pile of hardback books. If you have access to a paper press, then this is even better as the two boards can be screwed together and intense pressure can be applied from the shape to the paper.

EMBROIDERY OR APPLIQUÉ

This is an unusual way to give texture to paper, but now that papers are becoming more and more like fabric, with differing weights, sheens and pliability, they can be worked in the same way as fabric.

Occasional details can be added by hand sewing, but I would recommend using a sewing machine for embroidering on paper, because the stitches are very small and flat and therefore will not buckle the paper too much. Fine Japanese papers are perfect for this.

The same applies for appliqué, when a sewing machine is preferable for sewing paper motifs on a paper background. Although paper can also be appliquéd with glue, the textured effect of stitches around the edges of the pieces look much better.

CHAPTER **2**

The Home

Pencil Heaven

It is said that a chaotic desk can reflect a chaotic mind. If you are anything like me, your pens and pencils will be dotted all over the place and you can never find one – or at least one that works – when you need it. Keep them together by making this jazzy desk tidy, which takes minimum effort and gives maximum effect.

MATERIALS

Purple and turquoise rag paper

Thin card

Small plate or round template

Paper glue

Cellophane tape

Scissors

METHOD

1 Draw around the plate onto the card and cut it out. Then using this as a base, carefully tear two circles, slightly larger than the first card circle, from the purple rag paper. Sandwich the card circle in between the larger purple ones and glue the edges to close the card in – this will give the paper a stiff support.

2 Form three different sized cylinders from three rectangular pieces of card. Before you roll them into shape, snip tabs along the bottom edge of each piece and fold the tabs in all the way along, which will make them more stable when standing upright. Roll the rectangular pieces of card into cylinders and tape them into shape, ensuring that the tabs face inwards.

3 Before attaching the cylinders to the base, cover them in the turquoise rag paper. Tear the paper to give it a ragged edge and simply wrap it around the tubes, going no lower than the top of the tabs.

4 The last stage is to arrange the cylinders around the disc base – make sure they are all grouped together for maximum stability. Apply glue to the tabs at the bottom of the tubes and stick them to the base.

Square Storage

Being something of a box fiend, I like to use all shapes, sizes, colors and textures. The square box is the easiest to make and having made one, you will never be tempted to buy expensive cartons again. The method below uses the dimensions of the larger box from the three graduated sizes shown.

MATERIALS

85 x 60 cm (34 x 24 in) sheet of thick red embossed paper

85 x 60 cm (34 x 24 in) sheet of thick orange embossed paper

Thick card to use as a base

Ruler

Scissors

Pencil

Glue

Box measurements:

25 x 25 x 10 cm (10 x 10 x 4 in)

20 x 20 x 8 cm (8 x 8 x 3¼ in)

15 x 15 x 6 cm (6 x 6 x ¼ in)

METHOD

1 Cut a 25 cm (10 in) square out of the thick card to make a base for the box. Then make the box sides using the orange paper. As the paper is 85 x 60 cm (34 x 24 in), two strips are needed to go round all four sides. Cut two 52 x 12 cm (20½ x 4¾ in) strips. The extra 2 cm (¾ in) on each strip is for an overlap.

2 Glue the two strips together to make one long 102 cm (41 in) length, then mark 2 cm (¾ in) up along the bottom of the strip and rule a line running

straight across. Now measure and mark every 25 cm (10 in) along the ruled line and fold them at right angles to the ruled line to form four sides. Flatten the strip out and then fold up along the long ruled line and snip triangles out at the points where the folds meet.

3 Next glue the 2 cm (¾ in) turnups to the base of the box. Notice how the snipped triangles look neat and mitred and allow the sides to stand at right angles to the base as you work. Glue the 2 cm (¾ in) overlap on the side of the strip to the inside of the last free side.

4 Take the red paper to make the lid. This needs to be slightly larger than the base, so that it will fit comfortably and not too tightly. Cut a large square measuring 31.5 cm (12½ in) square, then measure in 3 cm (1⅛ in) on all four sides and rule lines along these measurements to make a smaller square inside the large one. Make four cuts from the edge of the large square to the edge of the smaller square at the four corners. Fold along the ruled lines and glue together the flaps at each corner.

Sunny Screen

Many of the papers available now are so soft and tactile that they feel and look like fabric, and can be embroidered in a similar way. The light shining through this paper blind also enhances the embroidered detail.

METHOD

1 Lay two sheets of embroidered paper together, at their shortest lengths, and glue them (see page 29 for embroidered paper). Cut the other two sheets in half lengthways and place them at each side of the two jointed piece. Glue together so that the width is increased. Rearrange to fit your window. Trim off the dowelling so that it fits perfectly along the top and bottom edges of the paper.

2 Place one of the lengths of dowelling at the top of the paper, turn the paper over so that the dowelling is caught inside and glue the paper down. Repeat with the second dowelling at the bottom, but this time lay the cord alongside, leaving two very long ends free at either side.

3 Measure out the distance needed between holes and punch holes up both sides of the paper at the same points. Using the hammer, attach the eyelets at the marked points. Then simply thread the cord through the holes up and over the top dowelling and back down (see Fig. 1).

4 Loop two hooks on the top of the blind to then attach to the window frame. Pull the blind up and down to get the correct folds in the paper. To tie it up, just knot the two lengths of card together.

Fig. 1

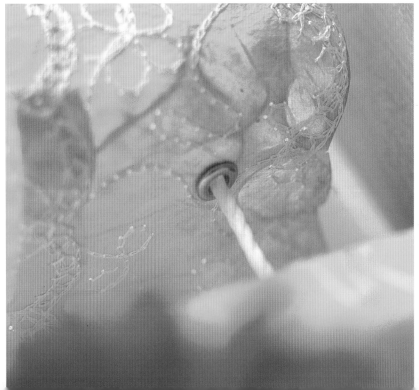

MATERIALS

4 sheets of yellow embroidered paper

2 lengths of 5 mm (¼ in) dowelling

Eyelets

Hammer

White cord

PVA or white glue

Ruler

Pencil

Golden Lanterns

These golden card nightlight shades were inspired by the lettering on sundials as well as by the metal light holders they are pictured with. When the candles are lit, the cast shadows of the cut shapes look most atmospheric when they fall against a plain wall. The templates used here include Roman numerals and star motifs, but you can just as easily design simple shapes of your own.

MATERIALS

Gold cardboard

Craft knife

Cutting mat

Pencil

Ruler

Glue

METHOD

1 Work out the grain of the card and ensure that the height follows the grain. These shades can be made to any size but the piece shown here uses a 7 cm (2¾ in) square. Measure 7 cm (2¾ in) up along the grain of the card and then 29 cm (11½ in) across. Mark off at every 7 cm (2¾ in) to form four sections and a 1 cm (⅜ in) allowance.

2 Cut out this strip and then fold at each 7 cm (2¾ in) interval to create four sides and one overlap. Snip the top and bottom of the overlap, so it is tidy when it is glued down.

3 Open the card out flat and then trace from the Roman numerals, sun or star templates (see page 106) onto the back of the card. Then, carefully cut them out, using a very sharp craft knife.

4 Fold the cube back up and simply glue the overlap onto the inside of the last edge. Pop a night light into the shade.

Note: Remember never to leave lighted candles unattended.

Mad Hatters

These round boxes are ideal for extra storage and can be used to put away all kinds of bits and pieces in a stylish way. They are suitable for anything, from socks and scarves to hats, toiletries and toys.

METHOD

1 Using a large, round tray or plate as a template, draw out two circles on the cardboard. Cut out one to its true size for the lid and one slightly smaller for the base.

2 Decide on the height you would like the box to be and mark this on the back of the paper. The height of the boxes shown here is 30 cm (12 in), 20 cm (8 in) and 10 cm (4 in). The length should be the same as the circumference of the base. Add a 2 cm (1 in) allowance onto the height and length and cut the shape out. Fold along the allowance line on the length, then flatten out and snip triangles onto the allowance (see Fig.1).

Fig. 1

3 Now begin to glue the triangle overlaps to the base, keeping the box sides at right angles to the base. Then overlap the two free sides and glue together. For extra strength tape along the inside join.

4 Make the lid in the same way as you made the base, snipping triangles into the allowance and easing the edges into place while gluing.

5 Place the lid face down on the paper, draw around the shape, cut it out and glue it on the top of the lid, covering the overlap. Then cut away any excess paper.

MATERIALS

85 x 60 cm (34 x 24 in) piece of cardboard

85 x 60 cm (34 x 24 in) piece of thick, shiny astrolux paper (sky-blue, eau-de-nil or cornflower)

Large circle for template

Scissors/craft knife

Strong glue

Sellotape

Ruler

Pencil

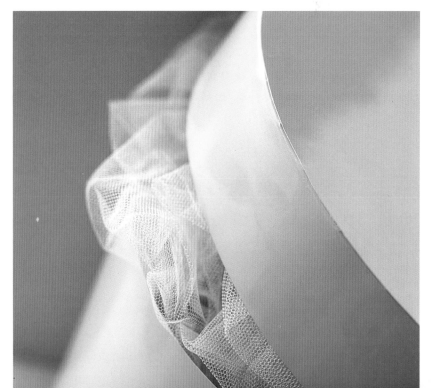

Red Wastebasket

This cheerful and practical wastepaper bin is made from two pieces of card, slotted together and fastened into place with paper fasteners. This is an ideal way of attaching the sides – with no gluing involved!

MATERIALS

- 85 x 60 cm (34 x 24 in) sheet of red corrugated card
- Smaller sheet of stiff red card
- Plate or round template
- Paper fasteners
- Tape measure
- Hole punch
- Craft knife
- Scissors
- Pencil
- Ruler

METHOD

1 For the base of the bin, draw around a plate onto the card and rule four lines around the circle to box it in to an exact square, touching the circle edges at four points. Mark eight equidistant tabs around the circumference of the circle by ruling four lines to segment the circle into eight (see Fig. 1).

2 Before cutting the card, wrap it around the plate or round template, leave an allowance for an overlap and cut off the excess card. Lay the card flat and cut at an angle along the top edge.

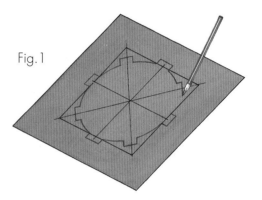

Fig. 1

3 Flip the card over so that the smooth side is facing up and rule a line across the card 2 cm (¾ in) up from the lower edge. Measure the circumference of the base, noting the distance between the tabs and each one's length and transfer these measurements to the line. Using a ruler and a very sharp craft knife, cut slits where the tabs would slot in.

4 Working around the base, slot the tabs into the slits and adjust the size of the slits where necessary. Mark on the card where the two upright free sides overlap. Unwrap the sides of the bin, then punch corresponding holes with the hole punch at equidistant points along the edge of the card.

5 Wrap the card back around the base and secure together the free edges with paper fasteners.

Zen Away

Screens can be so expensive to buy, but they are surprisingly easy to make, especially when using paper rather than fabric. This white and floaty paper screen will create a Zen-like atmosphere in your home.

METHOD

1 Make three frames measuring 150 x 75 cm (59 x 29½ in). Saw the corners at a 45 degree angle, so that they fit together neatly. Simply glue the corners together with the PVA and secure each corner with a panel pin. To toughen these joins, screw L-shaped plates on the reverse of each corner.

2 Attach three hinges on either side of each frame, 30 cm (12 in) from the top and the bottom. Then screw a frame on either side of the centre frame. Paint the frame with 2–3 coats of black gloss paint.

3 Lay the frames flat and lay the paper over the frames to work out where to trim them. About a third of a sheet needs to overlap onto the first, as one sheet will not cover an entire frame (see Fig.1). Then trim the paper to size.

4 Apply PVA glue neatly with a brush around the first frame and then ease the papers gently into place while the glue is still tacky. Gently stretch the paper taut, to avoid ripping the paper.

5 Screw black corner covers onto each corner joint for a neat finish.

MATERIALS

6 sheets of 120 x 85 (48 x 34 in) sized Japanese atsu unryu paper

6 strips of wood 4 x 4 x 150 cm (1½ x1½ x 59 in)

6 strips of wood 4 x 4 x 75 cm (1½ x1½ x 29½ in)

6 brass hinges and screws

12 black corner covers

12 L-shaped plates

Bradawl

Screws

Screwdriver

Hacksaw

Sandpaper

Panel pins

Hammer

PVA or white glue

Black gloss paint

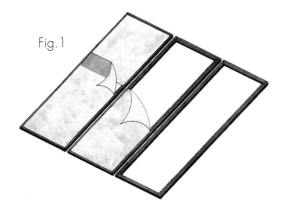

Fig.1

Checkmate

MATERIALS

Cylindrical
   lampshade
   frame
Blue and white
   tissue paper
Paper glue
Fire retardant spray
Ruler
Pencil
Scissors

This lampshade has been made with a basic paper weaving technique which creates a checkered effect. The baby blue and irridescent white tissue paper strips are woven in and out of each other and shimmer when they catch the light. Refer to page 27 for details of paper weaving techniques.

METHOD

1 Measure the circumference and height of the lampshade frame and cut strips of tissue at a width that will divide into those measurements. The white tissue is used vertically and the blue horizontally.

2 Begin with a strip of white tissue by securing one end to the top of the frame with glue. Then gently, but firmly, pull the strip taut and secure with glue to the lower edge of the frame. Secure the white tissue paper strips vertically all around the frame.

3 Once the frame is completely covered with vertical white strips, take a strip of blue tissue and, starting at the top of the frame, begin to weave it in and out of the white strips. When the free ends meet, attach them on the inside of the frame with a tiny dab of glue. Continue weaving the blue strips across the frame until it is filled.

4 Tidy up the edges of the frame, by gluing a strip of blue tissue over the top and lower edges, folding in the cut edges to give a smooth finish.

5 Finally spray the completed lampshade with a fine mist of fire retardant.

CHAPTER **3**

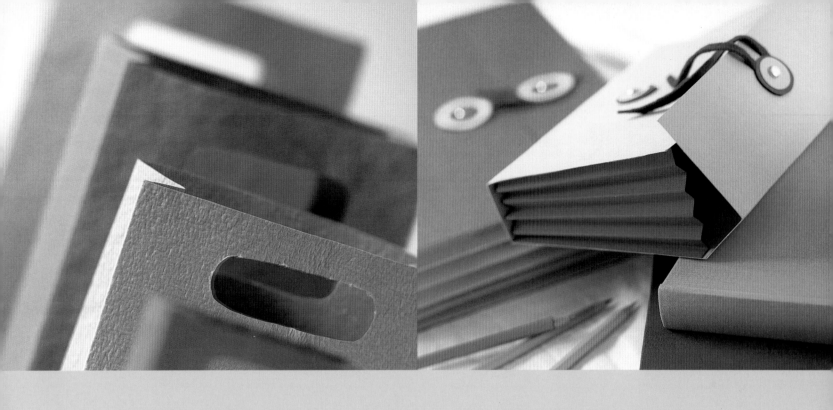

Stationery

Dream Letters

Make notepaper and envelopes to match by cutting them from one large sheet of paper using this embossing technique. This idea is most cost effective and also allows you to adapt the design and colors outlined here to suit your purposes.

MATERIALS

Navy and white
   cotton rag paper
Thick card or wire
Craft knife
Water spray
Roller
Heavy books or a
   paper press
Old blanket pieces
Flat board
Lo tack/tape
Cotton wool bud
Ruler
Pencil

METHOD
(for notepaper)

1 Cut the large sheet of cotton rag down to size. Then draw and cut out your chosen motif or letter from the thick card or twist your wire to shape. If you use wire, it needs to be at least 3 mm (⅛ in) thick. Now secure the motif onto the flat board, with lo tack or tape.

2 Spray the paper with the water spray, making it quite damp so that it is malleable, but not too wet. Put the paper over the board with the motif attached to it. Lay a couple of pieces of blanket over that and a heavy book on top of the pile. Use the roller to roll over the book, pressing the impression from the mold onto the paper.

3 Lay more heavy books on to the pile or close the paper into a paper press. Then leave for a couple of hours without disturbing it, until the paper has dried. After releasing the paper, you will find the motif embossed on it.

METHOD
(for envelopes)

1 Simply copy your choice of envelope template from pages 100–102 and trace this on the paper used for the notepaper.

2 Cut or tear out the shapes, fold along the dotted lines and glue the envelopes into shape.

Funky Files

Office folders and wallets in greys and browns can look so dreary and messy, so why not brighten up and tidy up by making your own? These portfolio cases in bright, acid colours look really stylish and are very simple to make. The dimensions for these instructions are designed to fit letter size papers, but you can adjust them to the size that you want.

METHOD

1 Cut the blue card into a rectangle measuring 35 x 69 cm (14 x 27½ in). Fold the card over a ruler at four points, at right angles to the long side. The first fold is made at a distance of 22 cm (9 in), the second at 5 cm (2 in), the third at 22 cm (9 in) and the fourth at 5 cm (2 in). This will leave 15 cm (6 in) for the overlap of the case. Make sure that the creases are sharp by pushing along the fold of the paper with the scissor handles.

2 Cut two pieces of green paper, each measuring 20 cm (8 in) square. Fold the paper with concertina folds at 2 cm (¾ in) intervals. Glue these to each side of the main body of the portfolio (see Fig. 1).

3 Cut two circles of green paper with a 4 cm (1½ in) diameter and two smaller circles of blue paper with a 2 cm (¾ in) diameter. Place each of the blue circles on a green circle and with a craft knife cut into the centers. Slot a paper fastener in to secure.

4 With a craft knife, mark the lower center of the portfolio flap and the main body of the folder, just below where the flap touches. Slot the paper circles and fasteners through these two points. Wind the felt strip or twine around the fasteners.

MATERIALS

Blue and green
    paper
Felt strip or twine
2 paper fasteners
Glue
Craft knife
Scissors
Pencil
Ruler

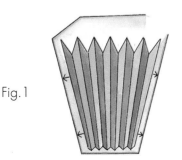

Fig. 1

57

Gift Glamour

MATERIALS

Giftwrapping
    papers
Tissue paper
Newspaper
Brown paper
Gold leaf
Dressmaker's wheel
Hole punch
Glue
Sellotape
Scissors
Pencil
Ruler

Having chosen the perfect gift, it makes a real difference if you can present it to suit the special occasion. There are so many ways of wrapping gifts of all sizes and here are included just a few with ideas for wrapping more unusual-shaped gifts on the next few pages.

METHOD
(for Gift 1 – see next spread)

1. Lay a sheet of newspaper out on a flat surface. One idea to make the paper look more unusual is to use a paper in a foreign language, such as Chinese or Arabic.

2. Mark off squares with a pencil around the whole sheet. Then paint in the squares with watered-down glue, lay pieces of gold leaf around the paper on the glued squares and allow them to dry. Use this gold-leafed paper to wrap your gift.

METHOD
(for Gift 2 – see next spread)

1. Lay a piece of brown paper onto a cutting mat and, using a craft knife, cut out small shapes from all over the sheet. You could choose to edge each cutout with a gold pen to highlight the 'windows'.

2. Now wrap the gift in a brightly colored tissue paper and cover it again with the brown paper.

METHOD
(for Gift 3 – below left)

1. Wrap your gift in a plain piece of paper. Then take a second piece of light paper, such as tissue paper, and pierce it with a dressmaker's wheel by running the wheel backwards and forwards over it.

2. Wrap this paper over the first and tiny dots of the first colour will show through.

Bags for All

These bags are so simple to make and are perfect for packaging an awkward-shaped gift in a colour to suit the occasion. Not only are there possible variations in the shape, but also in the types of paper. Choose to keep it simple with brown paper or newspaper, or experiment with metallics, gift wrap, tissue and handmade paper.

MATERIALS

Green and blue
   cotton rag paper
Craft knife
Glue
Scissors

METHOD

1 Copy the template from page 103. Draw around it, cut it out and then carefully cut out the oval shapes with a craft knife – these shapes will be the handles.

2 Fold in the bottom flaps and secure them together with glue.

3 The tags are simple, torn shapes with holes punched into the corners.

Note: The basic template could be adapted into alternative shapes, maybe shorter or wider ones and the shapes of the cut out handles could be varied – as circles, hearts or scallops.

Paper Greetings

Have you ever thought that you could make your own greeting cards? This is one of the best ways of working simply with paper, because all you need are leftover scraps of paper.

MATERIALS

Pink, blue and gold
   tissue paper
   scraps
A selection of gold
   and blue cards
Newspaper
Cartridge paper
Craft knife
Cutting mat
Paper glue stick
Ruler
Pencil

METHOD
(for Card 1 – page 66, right)

1 Cut a rectangular piece of stiff cream card to 17 x 22 cm (6¾ x 8⅝ in) and fold it in half so that the card is 17 x 11 cm (6¾ x 8⅝₁₆).

2 Tear strips of baby blue and turquoise tissue paper into strips, tearing along the grain for even strips and against the grain for more ragged strips. Crumple the baby blue tissue very tightly in your hand and then flatten it out.

3 Lay the strips across the card, vertically and horizontally, to make a checked pattern and glue them into place. Tear out small squares of tissue and stick them onto the card where the tissue strips overlap.

METHOD
(for Card 2 – page 67, centre)

1 Cut a rectangular piece of gold card to 16 x 22 cm (6¼ x 8⅝ in) and fold it in half so that the card is 16 x 11 cm (6¼ x 4 ⁵⁄₁₆ in).

2 Tear strips of newspaper and arrange them on the front of the card. Then tear up small squares of blue tissue paper, crumpling one of them into a tiny ball and then flattening it out to give it a soft texture.

3 Arrange these bits of paper around the card until you are happy with the composition and then glue them onto the card.

METHOD
(for Card 3 – page 67, right)

1 Cut a rectangular piece of cartridge paper measuring 15 x 30 cm (⅝ x 1⅛ in) and fold it in half to make a square card. Make sure you use a folding utensil to flatten the fold sharply.

2 Open it out and working on what will be the front of the card, use a pencil and a ruler to measure 1.5 cm (6 in) on all four sides of the card. Then work out how wide and how far apart you want the slits which will be used to weave the tissue paper.

3 Using a ruler and a craft knife, cut lines along the card and thread strips of tissue paper through the slits, securing with glue on the inside of the card.

in Jakarta
the top 15-20
0-plus banks
control mo
nt of bankin
nd rumours
ready gor
ossomed y
eculation th
are on the
st.
In neighbou
e ringgit fell
nt yester
ainst the d
ht fell 0.9 pe
pine peso,
se, droppe
nd the Sing
46 per cent.
'A new dy
leashed, t
ic way of
r value [d
s] right no
nk econor
rible and
of months
can judge
n get."
There is t
ird wave o
lity, and of
al fall-out f
ady appar

RE APR
E THE APR FOR YOUR PARTICULAR LOAN
RATE WILL BE THE SAME AS THE FIXED RA
UATION (WHICHEVER IS THE LOWER) AN A
CK OF 1% OF THE LOAN WILL BE PAID. MA
LOAN £20,000 APPLICATIONS RECEIVED A
INSTRUCT THE VALUER (PROCEDURE
BRANCH BY 13 DECEMBER 1997 A
THDRAW THIS MORTGAGE OFFER W
QUEST. FOR LOANS EXCEEDING
TO PRESS IN THE EXAMPLE USE
FOR ALLIANCE &

vay.

Lime Lozenges

You can make all sorts of packages for giftwrapping with the card or paper of your choice, be it store-bought or handmade. These lozenge-shaped boxes benefit from being made from a stiffer paper or card.

METHOD

1 Copy the templates on page 104 and draw around each one on a different colored card. Mark off the dotted lines for the folds and creases and then carefully cut them out.

2 All you have to do now is fold along the dotted lines, glue the long flap down and collapse the boxes into shape. Now you can fill them with gifts of your choice!

MATERIALS

3 shades of
  green card
Paper glue
Folding utensil
Scissors
Pencil

Papyrus Notes

Handmade books always look effective, especially when the paper they are made from is textured and tactile. The naïve qualities of the heavily textured papyrus and the Mexican bark paper work really well together.

MATERIALS

- 3 x 60 x 42.5 cm (24 x 17 in) sheets of papyrus paper
- 1 x 60 x 42.5 cm (24 x 17 in) sheet of brown Mexican bark paper
- Cotton twine
- Large needle
- Scissors
- Ruler
- Pencil

METHOD

1 Cut the first papyrus sheet into three equal rectangular sections. Repeat this with the other two sheets so that you have nine sections in total. Pile them on top of each other and fold them in half to make eighteen pages.

2 Lay the folded papyrus on top of the Mexican bark, fold this over the pages to make a cover and mark the size of the cover with a pencil. Remove the papyrus pages and tear the Mexican bark into shape, leaving an allowance all around the edge, so that the cover is larger than the pages.

3 Cut a strip of Mexican bark to the length of the spine of the pages and about 8 cm (3⅛ in) wide. Open the pages out flat and lay the bark centrally underneath the pile so that it lies down the spine. Sew running stitches through the centre middle pages, right through to the bark. When you reach the end, turn around and sew over the spaces that the running stitches have left (see Fig. 1).

4 Fold the pages back together, with the bark strip sewn onto the spine. Apply glue to the strip and stick it into the inside fold of the cover.

Note: Fig. 2 illustrates an alternative technique for creating pages with paper. Another idea is to buy hardback notebooks and simply cover them in papers of your choice, such as the leatherette covers shown here. Use a strong glue and keep the inside edges neat (see Fig. 3).

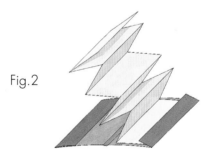

Fig.2

Fig.1

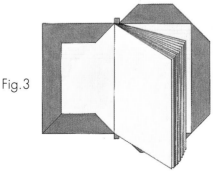

Fig.3

Wacky Wallets

This project covers a very basic technique of cutting and folding, providing an efficient – but also a bold and bright – paper storage. A medium-weight paper is a practical and attractive material to use for a project of this type.

MATERIALS

Medium-weight
   yellow and
   orange card
Elastic cord
Folding utensil
Hole punch
Scissors
Ruler
Pencil

METHOD

1 Copy the template shown here, either keeping it the same size or enlarging it, so that is suitable to carry letter size sheets of paper. Lay the template onto the card and draw around it. Mark off the dotted lines by ruling a line from both outside points.

2 Cut the shape of the wallet out with a strong and sharp pair of scissors. The card should be cut very straight, as there will be no overlap to tidy the sides up. Once you have cut the shape, then carefully bend and fold along the dotted lines.

3 Now the wallet has its shape, the points for the four holes should be marked and punched out (see Fig.1). Finally, thread a short length of elastic cord through the holes and knot them to keep them in place.

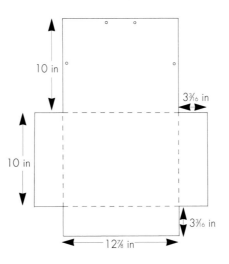

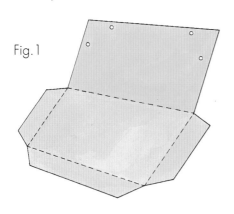

Fig. 1

CHAPTER **4**

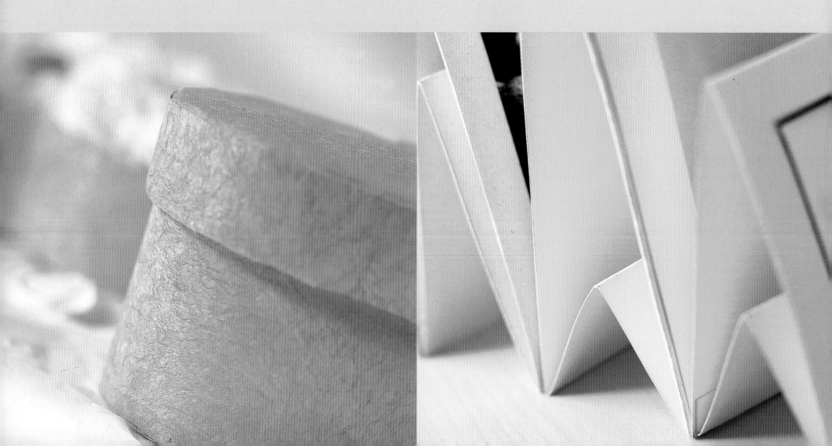

Accessories

Bonbon Boxes

Although these boxes are ideal for sweets, they can be used for any number of things apart from the traditional bonbons or sugared almonds. They could provide packaging for pieces of wedding or christening cake with name tags attached for each guest, or make a glamorous package for any miniature present.

MATERIALS

White astrolux paper – a 60 x 42.5 cm (24 x 17 in) sheet will make two boxes)

White tissue paper

White sheer ribbon

Hole punch

Strong glue

Scissors

Pencil

METHOD

1 Copy the template shown on page 105 and cut it out, marking the dotted lines. Work out which way the grain is lying in the paper and use this to your advantage (see Fiber and Grain on page 22). Place the template on the back of the astrolux paper and draw around it, again marking off the dotted lines.

2 Cut out the shape of the box and proceed to fold along all the dotted lines. The box will now start to take shape really quickly. Glue the flaps down to the inside of the base and the last side flap into the free side.

3 Take a hole punch and punch holes into the four peaks at the opening of the box. Line the box with tissue paper and then loop the ribbon through the two shorter sides and out through the two longer sides. Tie in an elaborate bow at the top.

Flower Dazzle

Artificial flowers often seem to try too hard to be real and as a result tend to become overly precious and old-fashioned looking. Why not go completely over the top with these huge, tissue paper flowers and revel in the artificial paper quality of these blooms? They are long-lasting, as well as flamboyant and fun.

METHOD

1 Leaving the wire on the roll while you are first working it, measure about 60 cm (23½ in) along and fold the wire in half. Work the second strand along the length and twist and fold it when you reach the end. Proceed to twist the wire once again around the double length to hold it in place, making the stem a triple thickness.

2 When you get to the top, loop the wire quite widely and twist off and cut the end. Then shape the wire to make a single lily flower (see photograph). Alternatively, to make a flower with petals falling to the side, take another length of wire and twist it into place, bending it over to one side.

3 Cut some green tissue paper into strips, tape it onto the bottom of the wire stem and twist it around and up to cover the entire stem. To make leaves, cut out elongated leaf shapes, with strips at the end and twist and glue them into position.

4 Choose brightly colored tissue papers for the petals and cut them to about three times the size of the loop at the top of the wire. Glue around the edges and just turn the edges over the loop, enclosing the wire in between two layers of tissue. You may need a couple of pieces of tissue paper to achieve a layered and folded effect.

5 While you are overlapping the tissue on the wire loop, gently pull the tissue along the wire, so that the tissue puckers and creases. Do not worry if it looks messy, as the build up of layers will hide any untidiness. Pull the end of the tissue around to the top of the stem and twist and glue it into place.

6 Green tissue paper will also look effective when wound around the base of each petal.

MATERIALS

Tissue paper in assorted colours
Roll of 2 mm (⅛ in) galvanised wire
Wire cutters
Paper glue stick
Scissors

Silver Style

Once you have made your artificial flowers (see page 81), then you need to think about how best to display them. To make them look even more dramatic, you could make a stylish paper vase to hold the flowers. When the vase is completed to your satisfaction a useful trick is to place some dry oasis in the bottom – this will weigh down the vase and hold the flowers in position.

METHOD

1 Draw around a small circular template on one side of the silver card for the base of the vase. Mark off every centimetre (½ in) around the circumference of the circle and make a small tab at every other mark and cut this out.

2 Take the rest of the card and wrap it around the circular template to check the size and then trim off the excess card, leaving an allowance for an overlap. Keep the vase at least 40 cm (16 in) in height, otherwise the flowers will droop over the sides.

3 Lay the card silver side down on a flat surface and measure 1 cm (½ in) up from the bottom and rule a line across the entire width. Mark off every centimetre (½ in) along this line. Then, with a ruler and craft knife, cut slits very carefully at every other point, so that the slits correspond with the tabs on the base disc.

4 Slot the tabs into their slits and mark off with a pencil where the paper fasteners will be placed. Unwrap the sides and punch holes along both free sides, every 2–3 cm (¾–1½ in). Replace the sides around the base and hold the sides together by fixing paper fasteners through the holes.

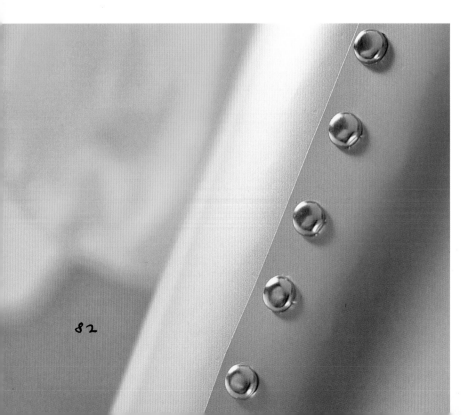

Picture Passion

These pictures are so simple to make and can create any number of unusual and creative effects. I have chosen a collection of collages inspired by Matisse, but the choice of color and texture of the paper really will dictate what you want to portray. The choice is yours, but remember that simplicity is the key for striking collages – use basic shapes and not more than four colours.

METHOD

1 Cut a piece of paper to fit exactly into the frame and then cut a piece in a contrasting colour, but slightly smaller, so that the picture will be mounted within the frame.

2 The collages shown use splash and leaf shapes in sky blue, royal purple and bright orange tissue papers. Use a selection of green tissues, crepes and foils, cut them into simple oak leaf shapes and arrange them on a contrasting background. Alternatively, experiment with weaving and create tartan and plaid effects with transparent papers, so that the colors change and overlap.

3 Arrange your chosen composition onto the cut paper. When you are happy with the image, simply glue the papers into position. If you are using fine tissue papers, it is advisable to use a spray mount adhesive, as glue sometimes shows through finer papers.

4 The next stage is to frame up your finshed collages – make sure that the frame suits the colors and textures that you have used.

Note: There are many unusual contemporary frames available to use with your collages, but these can be expensive. An alternative is to keep an eye out for old or unwanted frames in antique markets and sales. Even ordinary frames can be made to look interesting, when painted or distressed imaginatively.

MATERIALS

A variety of blue and white papers

Glue or spray mount

Small clip frames

Scissors

Heartfelt

A pretty, heart-shaped box covered in textured pink paper makes a lovely carton for a small Valentine's gift. It can be presented to your loved one as it is here, brimming with sweets, and then used as a box for holding little trinkets.

METHOD

1 Draw and cut out two heart shapes in the card (see page 107). The larger one will be the lid and the smaller one the base. Measure the circumference of the heart base and cut a strip of card slightly longer than this with a width of 7 cm (2¾ in).

2 Rule a line 1 cm (⅜ in) up from one long side of the strip and then snip tabs all the way along up to the line. Starting at the dip at the top, fold the tabs over the edge of the base and glue them down

firmly, ensuring that the 6 cm (2⅜ in) upright sides stay at a 90 degree angle to the base. At the end, overlap and tape the two upright ends together.

3 Do the same for the lid, but cut the strip so that it is 3 cm (1⅛ in) wide. This includes the 1 cm (⅜ in) edge for the tabs, making the lid side 2 cm (¾ in) high. Tape the tabs down for extra strength.

4 Now cover the box and lid with the Mexican bark paper. Cut a strip of the paper slightly longer than the base circumference and 8 cm (3⅛ in) wide. Rule in 1 cm (⅜ in) from the top and bottom lower edges, using these as a guide to snip tabs. Glue the paper around the box, using the tabs to ease the paper into position over the edges. Glue a heart shape to the base to cover the splayed tabs.

5 Cover the lid by cutting out a heart approximately 1 cm (⅜ in) larger than the lid all around, applying glue to the lid and pressing the paper down firmly. Once the paper is stuck, take the scissors and snip up to the edge of the heart all the way around the lid and glue the tabs down to the sides. Take a strip of paper and cover the sides in one smooth piece, hiding the tabs around the edges.

Sachet Scents

These square lavender sachets are a very simple project, using the technique of hand sewing on paper. The Japanese ichmatsu paper used here is so delicate and soft that it feels like fabric and can be treated as such. Just perfect for perfuming your drawers with a touch of style!

MATERIALS

Japanese ichmatsu paper

Dried lavender heads

Pinking shears or scissors

Sewing machine or needle

White cotton thread

Paperclips

METHOD

1 Cut out two identical pieces of tissue paper – simple shapes like squares and circles are ideal for this project. You could then use the pinking shears to give interesting detail to the cut edges.

2 The top sachet shown opposite uses cutouts of smaller shapes, graded in size and then sewn onto one of the pieces of paper. For this design, sew a few millimetres (about ⅛ in) in from the edges.

3 Take the back piece and lay the top piece into place. Proceed to sew together the pieces, with the sewing machine or by hand stitching. Remember only to sew three sides together.

4 Pour a handful of lavender heads into the sachet opening and simply sew the opening up.

Note: Apart from the checked and star patterns pictured here, Japanese ichmatsu paper is available in many variations, including wave and circle patterns and all come in a variety of colors and thicknesses. If you cannot find ichmatsu paper, photographic tissue or crepe paper have similar qualities.

Paper Memories

This hand-bound photograph album makes a wonderful keepsake to fill with photos and mementos. The soft lilac and green papers work well with the transparent tissue that inlays every page and protects the mounted photographs.

MATERIALS

60 x 42.5 cm (24 x 17 in) sheet of lilac bark paper

83.5 x 59 cm (33 x 23) sheet of photographic tissue paper

6 sheets of handmade fern notepaper

Lilac silk embroidery thread

Needle

Bradawl

Ruler

METHOD

1 Take one sheet of the notepaper and use this as a template on the photographic tissue. Cut out six pieces of the tissue to the exact size of the notepaper – there should be enough to make six sheets which will form the page inlays.

2 Cut or tear two pieces of the rag paper so that they are slightly larger than the pages and at least 7 cm (2¾ in) longer. These papers will form the front and back covers of the album.

3 Now lay one of the pieces of lilac paper on a flat surface and lay the first sheet of notepaper down, at least 5 cm (2 in) in from the left-hand side. Lay a sheet of tissue on that and then layer all the sheets one by one. Fold the left-hand side of the lilac paper forward and over all the pages to enclose them and hold them together.

4 Lay the front cover on top of the pile and line it up to the back cover. Fold over the extra on the left side towards the back. Measure points up along the left side at every centimetre (½ in), then take a bradawl and pierce holes at each mark, going through all the pages and both covers.

5 Sew through the holes, using a hemming stitch going one way, then turn around and go back in the opposite direction, so that they cross over each other (see Fig. 1). This will hold the book together.

Fig. 1

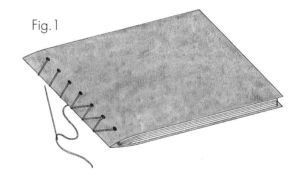

Note: A bradawl is an awl with a chiseled edge, available where papercrafting supplies are sold (see page 110).

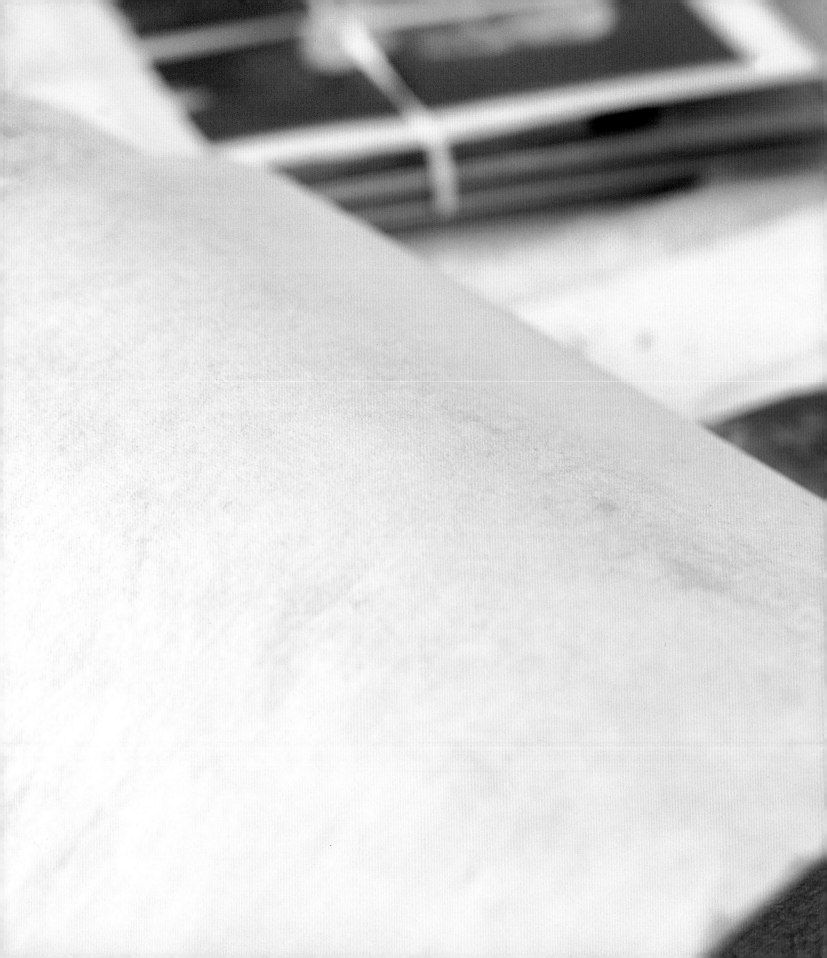

Folded Frames

These collapsible picture frames are really effective and can be made to any size. They are ideal for a collection of favorite postcards – choose the colors to complement those in the cards or in your interior.

METHOD

1 Work according to the measurements of the pictures to fit the frame. The inside frame of the picture frame has to be slightly smaller than the size you are framing, so it will secure the picture.

2 The postcard measurements here are 14 x 9 cm (5½ x 3½ in). The frame is 2 cm (¾ in) wide, so 4 cm (1⅝ in) were added, making the basic size a rectangle of 18 x 13 cm (7⅛ x 5⅛ in). Now cut out the three pieces that form the frame and its stand – a cartridge paper rectangle at 18 x 13 cm (7⅛ x 5⅛ in), another rectangle 2 cm (¾ in) in from this, leaving you with a frame (see templates on page 108).

3 Cut a length of paper 47 x 13 cm (18½ x 5⅛ in). Mark the length at 18 cm (7⅛ in), 18 cm (7⅛ in), 5 cm (1⅞ in) and 5 cm (1⅞ in), leaving you with 1 cm (½ in) at the end. Rule off these points with a soft pencil. Fold the length of paper at each of these points and glue the 1 cm (½ in) overlap on to the back of what will now be the stand (see Fig. 1).

4 Cut a frame with a slightly thinner thickness, using the same outside size as the first, but this one is three-sided, with the top left open. Glue this frame onto the main stand and the main frame on top of that. Then simply insert the postcard.

Fig. 1

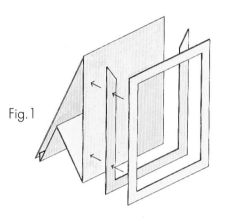

MATERIALS

Cartridge paper
Craft knife
Scissors
Paper glue stick
Ruler
Pencil

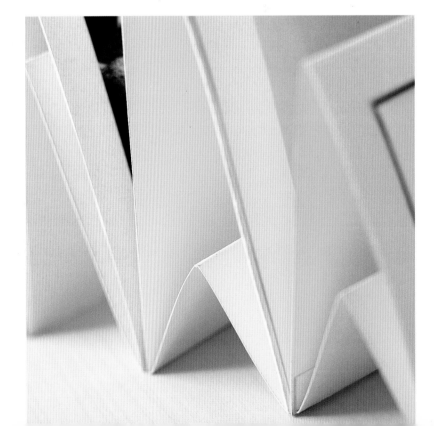

Celestial Boxes

Add some sparkle to your storage by making star-shaped boxes out of iridescent card. When the card catches the light it has a hologram effect, giving a really clean, modern look. These boxes are great as an alternative way to wrap smaller gifts – simply line the box with silver tissue paper for an extra surprise when the box is opened.

MATERIALS

60 x 42.5 cm (24 x 17 in sheet of iridescent card
Stiff card
Strong glue
Scissors
Pencil
Ruler

METHOD

1 Using the template on page 109, draw two stars onto the stiff card. Cut them both out, the larger one for the lid and the smaller one for the base. Each side of the star is 8 cm (3⅛ in) long and it has ten sides. The lazer card strip for the side has to be cut to a 9 cm depth (for the height of the box) and 82 cm (32¼ in) long, allowing for the extra 2 cm (¾ in) overlap.

2 Prepare the strip by ruling a line along its length 1 cm (⅜ in) up from the bottom edge. Fold the card along this line, creasing it firmly and then flatten it out. Rule lines at right angles to this fold at every 8 cm (3⅛ in) for the points of the stars, fold these over and flatten them out again. Snip small Vs at every other point where the folds cross.

3 Arrange the strip around the star-shaped base, folding the 1 cm (⅜ in) section under and gluing it around the star. Allow the larger section to stand upright and when you have glued down all the sides, fold in the extra 2 cm (¾ in) and glue into place on the inside of the box.

4 Repeat this process with the lid, but cut the width at 3 cm (1⅛ in), so that the lid edge will be 2 cm (¾ in) high with a 1 cm (⅜ in) overlap. Finally draw around the lid onto the back of the lazer card, cut it out so that it fits the top exactly and then glue it into place.

Templates

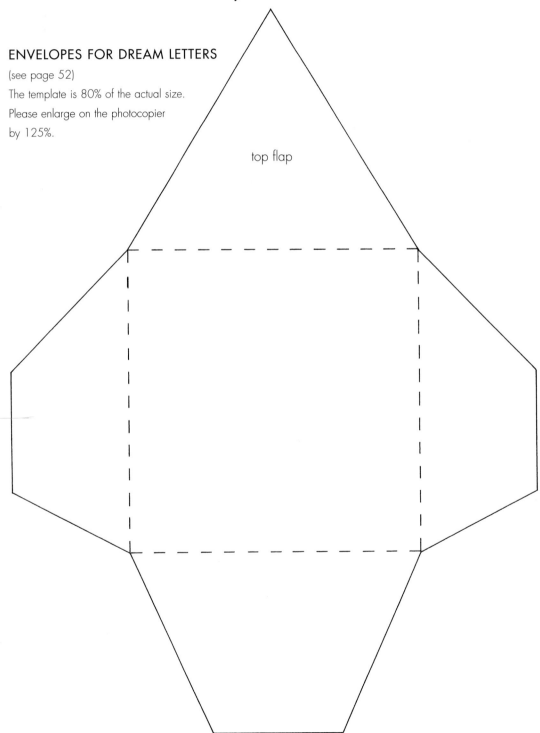

ENVELOPES FOR DREAM LETTERS

(see page 52)

The template is 80% of the actual size.

Please enlarge on the photocopier

by 125%.

top flap

100

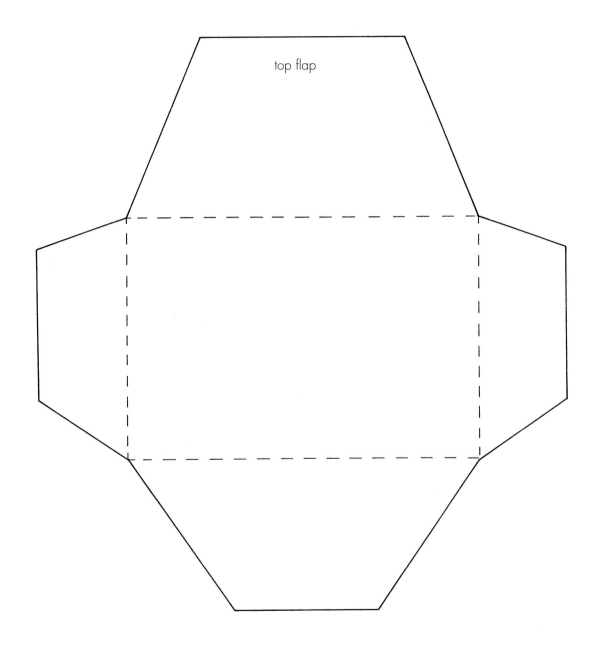

top flap

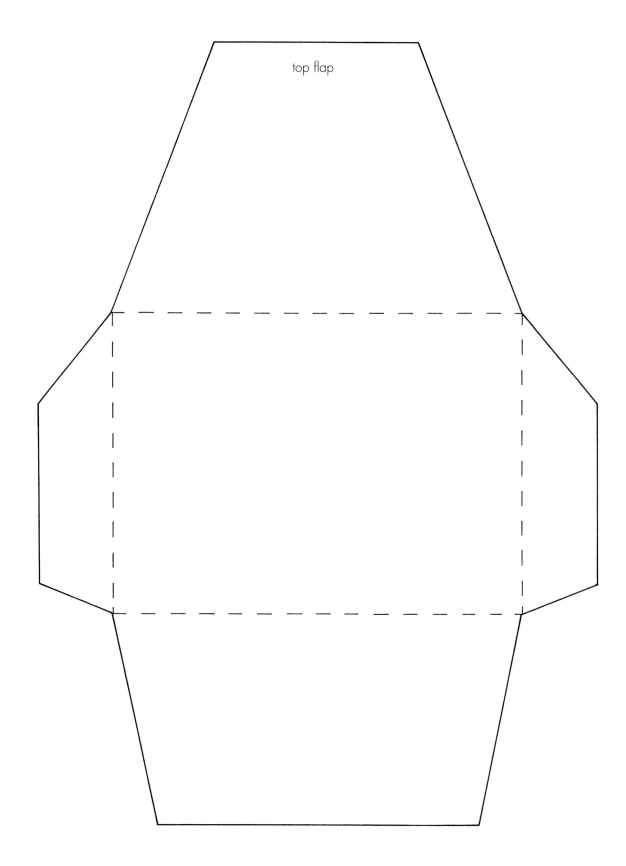

top flap

BAGS FOR ALL

(see page 63)

The template is 80% of the actual size. Please enlarge
on the photocopier by 125%. Alternatively reduce or
enlarge to your preference to create a range of sizes.

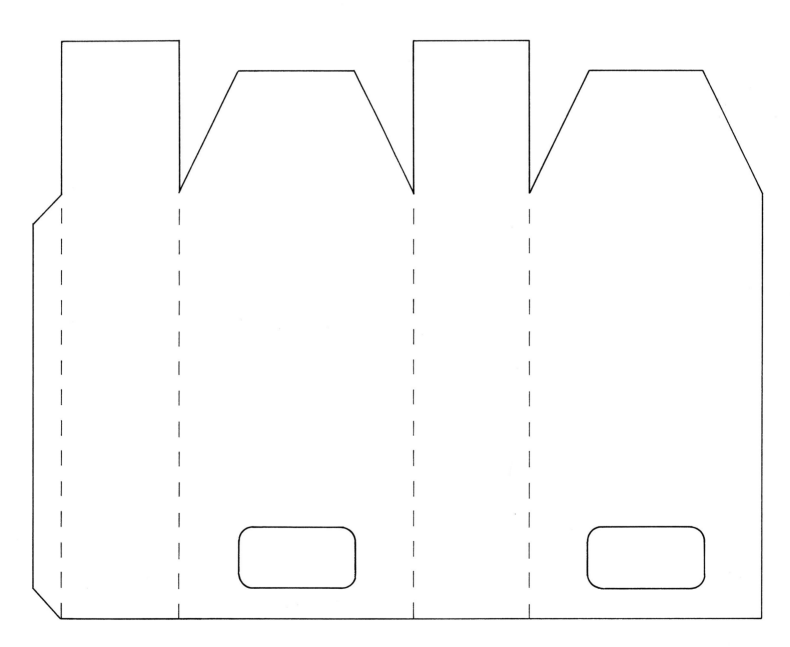

LIME LOZENGES

(see page 69)

This template shows the smallest size box – increase by
20% for the middle size and by 40% for the largest size.

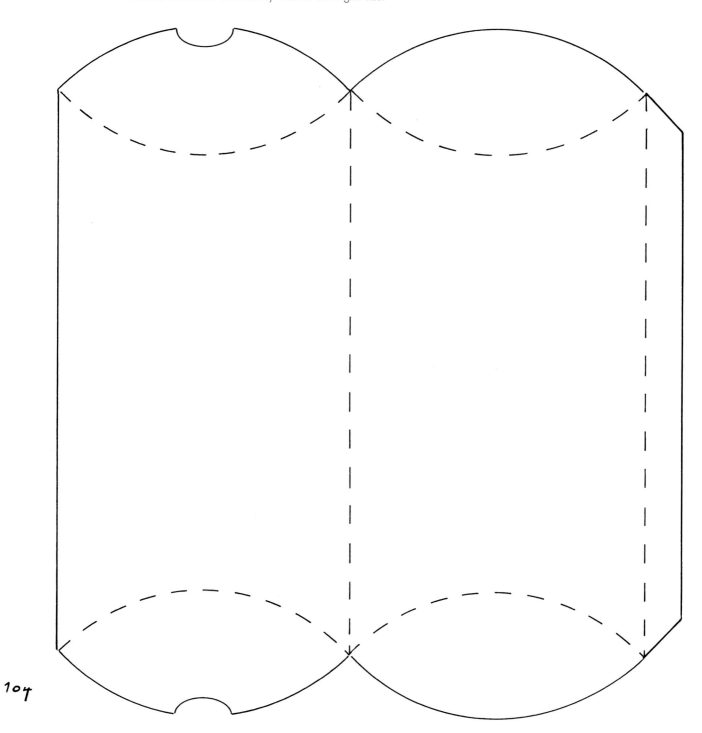

104

BONBON BOXES

(see page 78)

The template is 50% of the actual size. Please
enlarge on the photocopier by 200%.

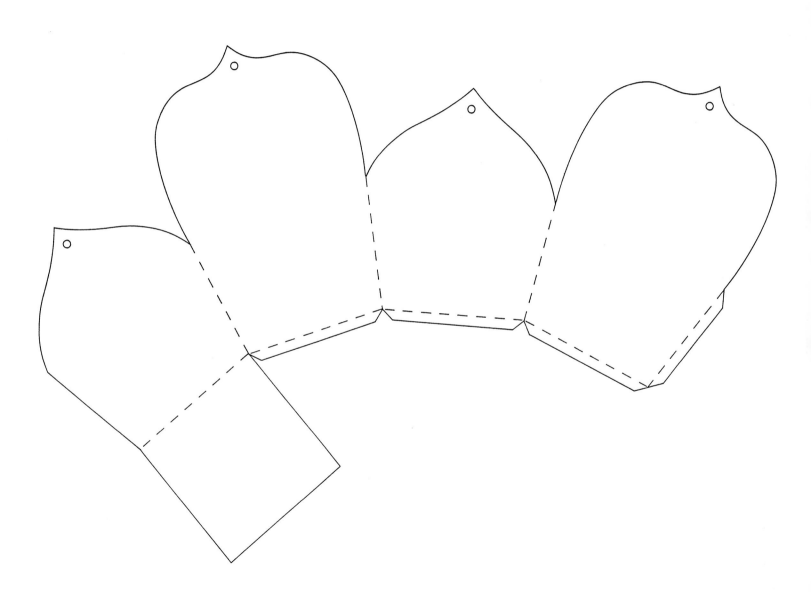

GOLDEN LANTERNS
(see page 38)

HEARTFELT

(see page 88)

Use larger heart for lid and smaller heart for base.

EMBOSSED MOTIFS FOR DREAM LETTERS

(see page 52)

FOLDED FRAMES

(see page 97)

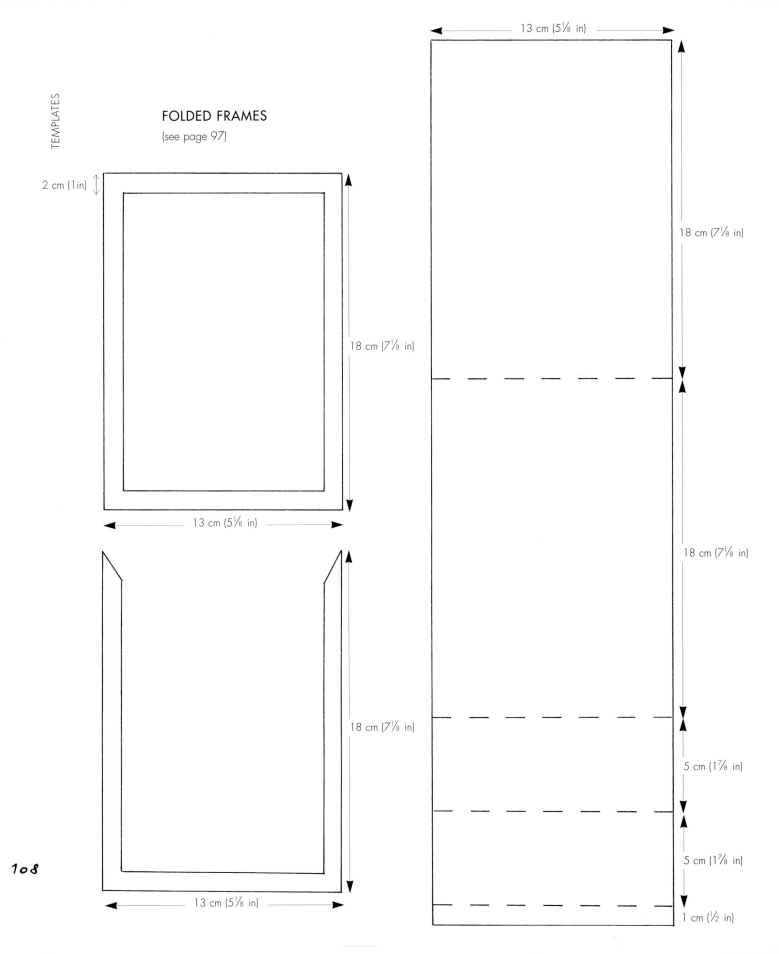

2 cm (1 in)

18 cm (7⅛ in)

13 cm (5⅛ in)

18 cm (7⅛ in)

13 cm (5⅛ in)

13 cm (5⅛ in)

18 cm (7⅛ in)

18 cm (7⅛ in)

5 cm (1⅞ in)

5 cm (1⅞ in)

1 cm (½ in)

108

CELESTIAL BOXES

(see page 98)

The template is 80% of the actual size. Please enlarge on the photocopier by 125%. Use the larger star for the lid and the smaller one for the base.

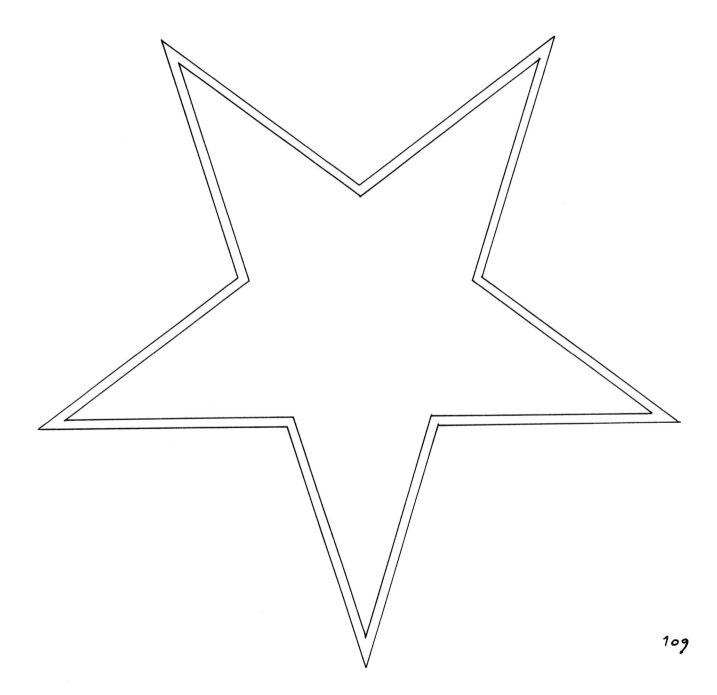

Suppliers

Most well-stocked craft stores and art-supply stores carry both elegant papers and most papermaking supplies, as well as tools and materials for decorating paper. In addition, a number of mail-order suppliers carry paper-related products. Below is just a sampling.

ASSORTED PAPERS/ART SUPPLIERS:

Aiko's Art Materials Import
3347 N. Clark St.
Chicago, IL 60657
(312) 404-5600
Japanese handmade papers

Daniel Smith, Inc.
4150 1st Avenue S
P.O. Box 84268
Seattle, WA 98124
(800) 426-6740

Fascinating Folds
http://www.fascinating-folds.com/
P.O. Box 10070
Glendale, AZ 85318
(800) 968-2418

Pearl Paint
http://www.pearlpaint.com/
308 Canal Street
New York City, NY 10013

Sax Arts & Crafts
P.O. Box 510710
New Berlin, WI 53151
(800) 221-6845

PAPERMAKING/BOOK-BINDING SUPPLIES:

The Bookbinder's Warehouse
31 Division Street
Keyport, NJ 07735
(908) 264-0306
Bookbinding supplies

Gold's Artworks, Inc.
2100 N. Pine Street
Lumberton, NC 28358
(800) 356-2306
Papermaking and bookbinding supplies

Lee Scott McDonald
P.O. Box 264
Charlestown, MA 02129
(888) 627-2737
Papermaking, bookbinding and marbling supplies

Magnolia
2527 Magnolia Street
Oakland, CA 94607
(510) 839-8334
Papermaking and bookbinding supplies

Twinrocker Handmade Paper
P.O. Box 413
Brookston, IN 47923
(317) 563-8946
Papermaking supplies

PAPERCUTTING:

Back Street Designs
P.O. Box 1213
Athens, AL 35611
Papercutting supplies

Gerlachs of Lecha
P.O. Box 213
Emmaus, PA 18049
Papercutting supplies

Simply Elegant Designs
2248 Obispo Avenue, Suite 206
Signal Hill, CA 90806
Papercutting and paper quilling supplies